ISBN: 1517769361
ISBN-13: 978-1517769369

Library of Congress Control Number: 2015917072
CreateSpace Independent Publishing Platform
North Charleston, South Carolina

The Cabin by the Riverside began as a poem written by Joseph Schmidt when he was eight years old. Along with the words of the poem, Joseph created a vivid inner landscape which brought the poem to life in his mind. The poem and these images remained close to him throughout his life and became a bed-time prayer for his children. Later in life, Joseph decided to capture these images for a children's book and sketched each scene as he saw it in his mind's eye. He then worked with June Atkin, a professional illustrator, who followed these sketches to render the finished scenes that you find in this book.

The Cabin by the Riverside

by
Joseph Schmidt

Illustrated by June Atkin

The cabin by
the riverside is getting
old and gray

8

It's small and
sort of shabby

But
warm
in
every
way

Burning embers in the hearth
Give light throughout the room

While Father tells us stories
My Mother weaves the loom

At night before we go to bed
We kneel down to pray
With thankfulness for all that's kept us
Safe and warm throughout the day

Thank you for
the Earth...

Trees...

and Animals

Thank you for
the Sun...

Moon...

and Stars

Thank you for
Work...

Thank you for Food...

and Water

Thank you for Light...

and Warmth

And most of all...

Thank you for
the love we share

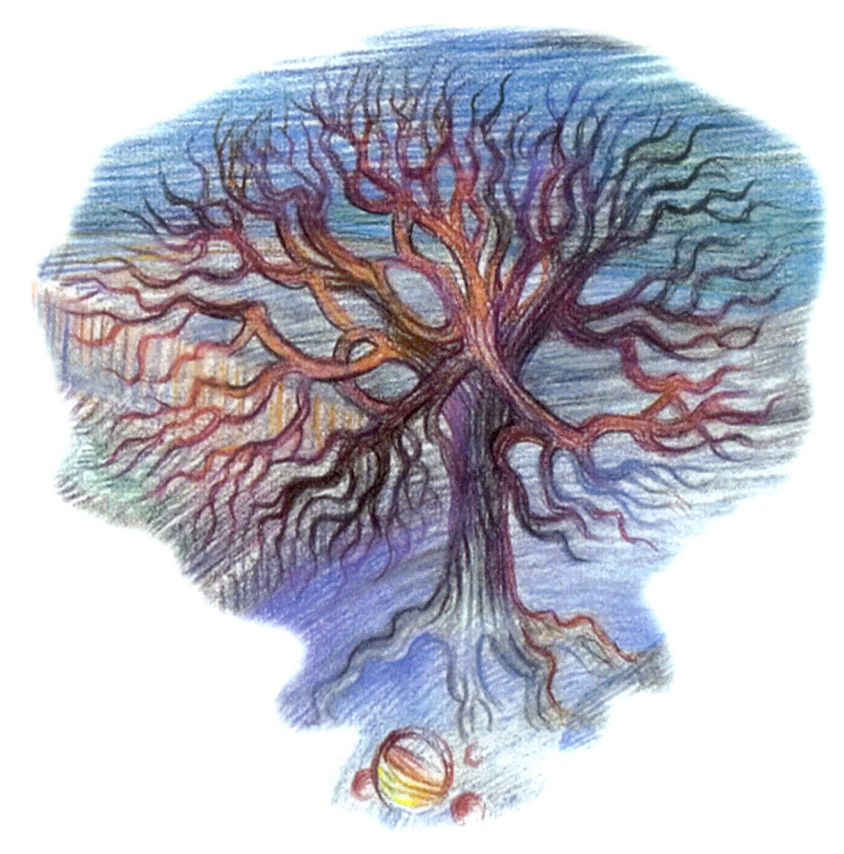

Also by Joseph Schmidt:

THE TORCHBEARER

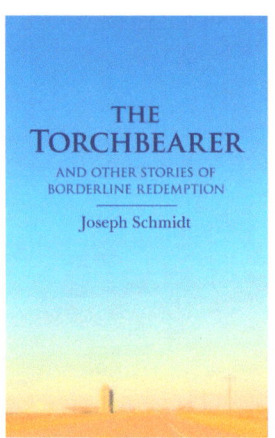

Explore the unknown in Joseph Schmidt's lyrical new collection, The Torchbearer. Through the course of these unique and enchanting stories, readers will enter into a subtly haunting world filled with people and places that will not soon be forgotten.

Each tale comes alive with intriguing characters that offer a glimpse into a reality that is both the same, and delightfully different, from our own. This engaging collection will lead readers to unexpected destinations as they journey through the intricacies of their own hearts.

Praise from Kirkus Reviews:

"Twenty-one short stories—some surreal, others unsettling, several ineffably beautiful."

"Rod Serling could have given a Twilight Zone intro to each story in this collection."

"Set mostly in the present day, the stories' many varied locations range from Tribeca to Kansas to an enchanted garden. Narrators vary too—in age, sex and authority—but all experience a change that may take readers by surprise."

"A winding journey into a wondrous land of imagination."

www.torchbearerstories.com
Available on Amazon